COOPERATIVE EXTENSION WORK

IN AGRICULTURE AND HOME ECONOMICS

STATE OF OKLAHOMA

W. A. CONNER, Director

OKLAHOMA AGRICULTURAL AND MECHANICAL

COLLEGE AND UNITED STATES DEPARTMENT

OF AGRICULTURE, COOPERATING EXTENSION

SERVICE COUNTY AGENT WORK STILLWATER,

OKLAHOMA

Distributed in Furtherance of the Acts of

Congress of May 8 and June 30, 1914

Curing Pork on the Farm

By Fred J. Beard

Circular No. 220 General Series 58

ISBN-10   1511644362

ISBN-13   978-1511644365

Table of Contents

Curing Pork on the Farm

By Fred J. Beard

Home curing of pork is an old practice. In early farming days, home curing of meats was an occupation in which all the better farmers took a pride. It was a measure of success and each farmer tried to excell his neighbor in the dressing and curing of the year's supply of meat. Curing pork nearly went out of style but the style is rapidly becoming popular again. Farmers can supply their own meat with as good flavor as that found in meats which are purchased at the markets and at a lower cost than that demanded in the city markets.

Winter is the most satisfactory time for butchering because the spring pigs are in good condition for slaughter at this season and farm work is usually not so urgent. The meat is more easily preserved in either the fresh or cured state at this time of the year. It doesn't require an elaborate set of tools and equipment to do farm butchering. The tools and equipment that are to be used should be put in readiness before butchering starts. It is essential to have the proper equipment for rapid and skillful work at killing time. They are: 8 inch butcher knife, meat saw, 14 inch steel, hog hook (heavy hay hook will do), bell scraper, and a gambrel (a single-tree will suffice). A barrel tilted at about 30° to 45° angle makes a good scalding vat. A platform laid on 4" x 4"s to hold it out of the water and mud makes a good place on which to scrape the hog. Provide a place convenient to the platform to hang the hog to dress. This may be only a tripod or a strong post extending about 8 feet above the ground on which one or two cross arms are bolted. This will accommodate several hogs.

Selection

In selecting hogs for butchering, health is the first consideration. Do not select any animal that appears "off." Meat spoils easily if the animals are in the slightest diseased condition. Then too, there is always that danger of transmitting disease to the consumer. It is not always just enough to inspect the hog while alive but while dressing the carcass look carefully for diseases, especially tuberculosis and hog cholera. Injured animals should be butchered at once but it will be necessary to pare away .the parts affected.

Hogs weighing 200 to 250 pounds in medium condition and gaining in weight make the ideal kind for butchering. Do not kill a hog if losing in weight as the meat is apt to be tough and lacking in flavor and juiciness. Meat from very young hogs lacks flavor and is watery, while that from old hogs usually is tough. Hogs can be killed any time after 6 weeks but generally better success will be had curing meat from hogs 9 to 12 months old. Boars, if castrated and fattened after they have healed, will lose most of that strong odor and flavor. The quality of such meat depends on the age and smoothness of the animal.

Keep animals off feed for 24 hours prior to slaughter. This promotes elimination of waste products from the system and also aids in emptying the stomach and intestines of their content which makes dressing the carcass easier. Whipping or beating animals before slaughter impairs the keeping qualities of the meat.

Methods of Slaughter

The animals may be shot or stunned before they are stuck but ordinarily it is not necessary. Shooting kills the hog and stops the flow of blood. Stunning is a cruel method as one is too apt to miss his mark. With the aid of two hurdles, drive the hog near the place of scalding. Two men reach beneath the hog and grasp the legs on the opposite side and with a quick jerk roll the hog on to its back. One man steps astride the animal with his legs just back of the hog's shoulders and in close to the body, at the same time holding to the fore legs. In this position, the hog is easily held while the other man does the sticking.

Take the knife and make an opening through the skin from the breast bone half way down the throat. With the cutting edge down, run the point of the knife three-fourths of an inch below the point of the breast bone and push straight down to the neck bone. Draw the knife out extending the incision on the neck to allow freer passage of the blood. Be sure the hog lies squarely on its back or one is likely to stick the shoulder. Hold the jaw down with one hand while sticking the hog with the other. It is not advisable to stick the heart as it will pump nearly all of the blood out if not pierced. After sticking, let the hog up but it should not be allowed to run away as it will necessitate carrying it back to scald. Have the blood flowing freely before turning the hog loose. The animal will be unconscious in one or two minutes after sticking. The kicking and scrambling which the hog does after sticking is a good thing as it facilitates bleeding.

Scalding and Cleaning

A very important thing in scalding is to have the temperature of the water right. The water should be heated near the place where the hog is to be scalded. It may be heated in the house but should be boiling when removed from the stove. It will require about one-half barrel of water. The best temperature is about 150 degrees Fahrenheit. The most accurate way to test is with a thermometer but in absence of one, test the temperature by dipping a finger in the water three times in rapid succession. It should burn severely the third time. If it burns severely the first time, the water is too hot. It is preferable to have the water a little too cold than too hot. There is always danger of setting the hair when scalding with water that is too hot. Hair that is set has to be shaved off and the carcass never looks as nice nor as clean.

The addition of a small shovelful of wood ashes, handful of airslaked lime, teaspoonful of lye or a bar of soap to the water aids greatly in removing the hair and scurf and leaves the hog's hide much whiter and cleaner. After adding either of these, the water should be stirred. The addition of too much lye or lime with water that is too hot will cook the hide until it comes off in chunks when scraping.

Place the hog on the platform to be scalded. Roll the hog on to its belly and spread the legs well apart. One man lifts the fore legs while another lifts the hind part by holding the legs well apart to balance the hog. In this way, two men can lift a 250 to 300 pound hog with comparative ease.

The rear end of the hog should be scalded first for the reason that if the Water should be too hot and sets the hair, it will be easier to remove from the rear end than from the front end. Insert the hook in the lower jaw and push the hind part of the hog into the barrel. With the aid of the hook and fore legs, keep turning the hog in the barrel to avoid having one side lay too long against the side of the barrel thus failing to scald. It is not necessary that the hog be drawn out only to try the hair. When the hair slips freely on the hams and legs, draw the hog out of the barrel and with the hands quickly twist the hair from the legs, cut out the gambrels, put in the gambrel stick and scald the fore end. When properly scalded, draw the hog out on the platform or table and scrape the fore end as quickly as possible. The head and neck are much harder to clean after they have cooled than the hind part. The hog should be scraped as quickly as possible as the hair never slips as easily after it cools once as it does when first taken out of the water, even though warmed up by pouring hot water over the hog. If the hog is very large, it may not scald around the fore flanks. Cover the unscalded parts with some loose hair and pour on hot water. It is possible to scald all of a hog by covering with hair and burlap sacks, then pouring on the water.

After the hog is scraped, hang and rinse with hot water. Scrape down well to get any hair and scurf that remains. It may be necessary to repeat several times to get the hide white and clean. Any hair that remains should be shaved off with a knife. Then rinse with cold water, and with the back edge of a knife scrape up on the hog to close the pores and squeeze out any remaining dirt. This leaves the hide dry and clean.

Dressing the Hog

The next step is to remove the entrails. Cut down between the hams to the aitch bone and split the skin along the mid-line to the head. Holding the knife blade, cutting edge up, place the point on the white seam of the aitch bone and tap the handle lightly with the other hand which drives the knife along the seam, thus splitting the aitch bone. To loosen the bung, pull it forward and upward at the same time cutting it loose on the sides and behind it. Tie it off with a string. Open the belly to the breast bone. A very quick and easy way to do this is to place the hand inside the abdominal cavity and while grasping the handle of the knife, force the hand down, splitting the belly with the heel of the knife. Roll all of the intestines, the stomach and liver out into a tub. Cut the esophagus about two inches in front of the stomach. This removes all the viscera from the abdominal cavity.

To open the chest cavity, insert the knife, cutting edge up, in the place where the hog was first stuck but extending the point into the cavity. Pull up on the handle allowing the point of the knife to rest on the back bone, thus splitting the breast bone with the heel of the knife. Then cut the diaphragm and remove the heart and lungs. The tongue should be removed at this time if the head is to remain on the carcass. Any blood or soiled places on the carcass should be washed off before it dries.

Remove the liver by running the thumb underneath the bile duct and peeling the gall bladder away from the liver. Cut the liver loose from the intestines, wash and hang up to cool. The heart should be removed, and the blood washed out with cold water.

The carcass should be split down the center of the backbone to the nose with a saw or a cleaver. It takes only one trial to convince anyone that splitting with a saw is superior to hacking the backbone out and tearing the loin to pieces. Loosen the leaf fat while the carcass is still warm as it comes out much easier. Start loosening at the bottom by separating the layer of fat from the inside muscles of the belly. The kidneys may be left in the leaf fat until later. Another advantage in loosening the leaf fat at this time is that it hastens cooling of the carcass.

Cutting and Trimming

The carcass should be allowed to cool thoroughly before it is cut, but not allowed to freeze. Much neater job of trimming can be done after the meat is chilled. A very desirable temperature for cooling meat is 34 to 36 degrees F.

Lay half of the carcass on a table or box with the bone side up. Take the head off at the atlas joint which is about one inch back of the ears. The cut should be made at right angles to the carcass so as to leave the shoulder square. The fat of the head is used for lard, and the lean for sausage or headcheese. The jowl is sometimes given a light cure and used for cooking with vegetables.

The shoulder is removed by cutting back of the third and across the fourth rib which is about one or two inches behind the elbow. This makes a cut parallel with the neck cut, giving a rectangular shaped shoulder. Remove the neck bones and ribs by cutting as close to the bone as possible. Care should be taken not to cut into the shoulder with the point of the knife. Trim the shoulder by cutting away all ragged edges and excess fat. Rounding edges are preferred to square ones. All of the bloody meat should be trimmed off. Cut the shank off above the knee at right angle to the bone. If only a small quantity of cured meat is desired or if the shoulders are too large to cure (18-20 lbs.), the top of the shoulder may be taken off. Begin where the neck bone came out and cut parallel with the top of the shoulder. The lean portion of this "shoulder butt" may be used for sausage or as a roast and the fat put into lard.

Middle Piece. The ham is removed by sawing at right angles to the shank and about two inches in front of the aitch bone. This makes the cut across the back bone four or five bones back of where it starts to raise toward the tail. The exact distance in front of the aitch bone is variable depending on the size of the hog. If the hog weighs less than 200 pounds the ham can be cut a little longer but if the hog weighs 300 pounds or more the cut should be made close to the aitch bone. Large hams and shoulders are more difficult to cure.

The back is cut from the belly by starting just below the turn of the rib at the front of the middle piece and barely missing the tenderloin muscle at the rear end. This makes a cut almost parallel with the back line. Separate the back fat from the loin being careful to leave about one-fourth inch covering of fat on the loin. The back fat goes for lard and the loin as pork chops or roasts. It may be given a sprinkling of salt, laid on the curing meat and kept for several days if the weather is cool.

Trim the spare ribs out of the belly by cutting as closely as possible to the bones. Turn the belly over with skin side up and press out the wrinkles and folds. Square up the edges and use for bacon.

Trim the ham up smoothly exposing as little lean meat as possible. If excessively fat, skin the ham leaving about one-half inch layer of fat on the lean. Cut the shank off above the hock.

Making Sausage

All lean trimmings should be ground for sausage. The lean should be separated rather closely from the fat. Too much fat in the sausage meat will cause it to fry up too much while lean meat in the fat will cause the lard to render out dark. Pork for sausage should not be over one-fourth fat. One pound of salt, 2 ounces pepper and 3 ounces of sage, if desired, to 50 pounds of meat makes about the right seasoning. The seasoning may be mixed with the meat before or after grinding.

Rendering Lard

Cut all the fat in one or one and one-half inch cubes to render. If the hog was not thoroughly cleaned, it would be advisable to remove the skin as the dirt in the hide will make the lard taste strong and sometimes cause it to get rancid rather quickly. Do not render the gut fat with the other fat.

Pour about one-half gallon of water into the rendering kettle and fill nearly full with fat cuttings. Cook over a moderate fire and stir frequently to prevent sticking to the kettle. When the cracklings begin to brown and to float it should be stirred continuously to get all pieces cooked properly. There will be a great mass of white bubbles on the top and blisters will form · on the cracklings. When nearly all of the white bubbles are cooked off and the cracklings when lifted out fry themselves dry, the lard is finished. Remove the kettle from the fire and allow the lard to cool a little, then strain through a muslin cloth into containers previously cleaned and dried. Lard obtained from squeezing the cracklings should be placed in a separate container as it will contain more sediment and likely be a little darker. Stirring the lard as it cools tends to whiten it and make it finer grained. Store in a cool dark place that is dry and well ventilated. When using from a vessel, remove it evenly from the surface or it will become rancid.

Head Cheese

Trim all meat from the head. Boil with heart, tongue, tail and feet until meat can easily be separated from the bones. Pour off the liquid and take out all the bones and tear the meat apart. Season to taste, cover with the liquid and boil a few minutes longer. Pour the mixture into a shallow pan and weight down. When cool, take off the grease and the meat is ready to serve.

Scrapple

Use the same kind of meat and proceed the same way as with head cheese. After the meat is seasoned pour back all the liquid and start heating it. Begin adding corn meal slowly and stir constantly until mixture is about as thick as corn mush. Boil until the corn meal is cooked and pour into shallow pans to cool. It can be sliced and served cold but is much better if fried.

Curing Pork

Meat, before it is put into cure, should be thoroughly cooled out but never allowed to freeze.

There are two general methods of curing meat-dry cure and brine or pickle: In Loth cures, sugar is recommended with other ingredients which accounts for it being spoken of as sugar cure and distinguished from plain salt cure. The ingredients for curing are: salt, saltpeter, and sugar or molasses.

Salt and Sugar Better. Salt is the basis of all meat curing. When applied to meat alone, it makes the meat very hard and dry because the action of the salt draws out the meat juices and hardens the muscle fibers. Sugar or molasses act differently than salt. They tend to soften the muscle fibers as well as to improve the flavor. Saltpeter is used to retain the natural color of the meat, but should be used very sparingly.

Curing Vessels. Common, clean, hardwood molasses or syrup barrels furnish suitable vessels in which to cure pork. A large stone jar is the best container but the initial cost is high, the jars, difficult to handle and are relatively easily broken.

Place to Cure. Meat can be cured in a well ventilated cellar or in a smoke house. Do not expect the best product if exposed to dirt and dust while curing or after smoking. The meat should not be allowed to freeze while curing.

It is easier to get a uniform cure with the brine method but generally not so satisfactory in mild winters as the brine sours and the meat spoils. The meat can often be saved, if sour brine is noticed early and drained off. The meat should be washed and new brine added. Excellent results may be obtained with the dry cure if care is taken to get the cure rubbed on evenly. Dry cure is safer if the weather is warm.

Brine Cure. Make a mixture as follows for each 100 pounds of meat:

8 lbs salt

2 1/3 lbs. sugar

2 oz. saltpeter

4 gallons water

or

12 lbs. salt

3 lbs. sugar

2 oz. saltpeter

6 gallons water

In warm weather two more pounds of salt are preferable. Allow 4 days' cure for each pound in the ham or shoulder and three days for bacon and. small pieces.

For example, a 15-pound ham should stay in cure 60 days while a 10-pound bacon remains in cure only 30 days. The water which makes up the brine should be boiled to insure its purity. This should be done the day before the water is to be used so as to allow ample time for it to cool.

Placing Meat in Brine Cure. Weigh out the ingredients and mix well. Rub the meat with the mixture, shake off the surplus and pack loosely in the curing vessel. Place the hams on the bottom of the container, shoulders next, bacon and smaller cuts on top. Dissolve the remainder of the curing mixture in the water and pour over the meat, being sure that the meat is well covered. It will be necessary to weight meat down to prevent floating. The meat should be repacked in 5, 10 and 15 days respectively, each time reversing the location of the meat in the container. When each piece has had the proper cure, take it out, wash in warm water, string and hang to drip, then smoke.

Dry Curing. For each 100 pounds of meat, weigh out the following:

8 lbs. salt

2 ½ lbs. sugar

2 oz. saltpeter

Rub about one-half of this mixture thoroughly on pieces and pack in a box or barrel. On the seventh day, take out meat and rub remainder of mixture on meat and repack. Allow to cure 3 days per pound in each piece. When cured, remove, brush and smoke.

Do Not Use Pine Wood for Smoking

Green hickory, maple, apple or even corn cobs may be used. Resinous woods should never be used as they deposit carbon on the meat and give an objectionable flavor to the meat. Space the meat in a smoke house to insure good circulation of the smoke. After the meat has hung for 24 hours, a slow fire should be started and kept going continuously until meat has a rich amber to medium brown color. Smoking helps to preserve meat as well as give it a desirable flavor.

Wrap the Meat. Smoked meat should be wrapped in heavy paper and sewed in muslin sacks. This prevents drying out and getting hard. Cut all strings off the meat before it is placed in the sacks, as the meat cannot be made vermin proof if hung by these old strings. Each sack should be painted with a yellow wash and hung up for future use.

Yellow Wash. The following yellow wash is recommended in the U. S. Farmers' Bulletin 1186. For 100 pounds wrapped meat use:

3 lbs. barium sulphate

1 oz. of dry glue

1 ¼ oz. chrome yellow

6 oz. flour

Thoroughly mix the flour in a half pail of water. Mix the chrome Yellow in a quart of water in a separate vessel, add the glue and pour both into the pail containing the flour and water mixture. Bring the whole mixture to a boil and add the barium sulphate very slowly, stirring constantly. Allow to thoroughly cool and apply with a brush but stir it frequently while using it.

www.ingramcontent.com/pod-product-compliance
Lightning Source LLC
Chambersburg PA
CBHW070525290526
45790CB00003B/1301